Dizzy Spell

Dizzy Spell

◆

Living & Coping with an Inner Ear Disorder

Gillian Gabrielle Barnett

iUniverse, Inc.
New York Lincoln Shanghai

Dizzy Spell
Living & Coping with an Inner Ear Disorder

Copyright © 2005 by Gillian Gabrielle Barnett

All rights reserved. No part of this book may be used or reproduced by any means, graphic, electronic, or mechanical, including photocopying, recording, taping or by any information storage retrieval system without the written permission of the publisher except in the case of brief quotations embodied in critical articles and reviews.

iUniverse books may be ordered through booksellers or by contacting:

iUniverse
2021 Pine Lake Road, Suite 100
Lincoln, NE 68512
www.iuniverse.com
1-800-Authors (1-800-288-4677)

ISBN: 0-595-34044-X

Printed in the United States of America

This book is dedicated to
All the people who had and are still having a
"Dizzy Spell"

"See to live is to suffer but to survive, well that's to find meaning in the suffering."

—DMX

Contents

Introduction 1
Balance as a Sixth Sense. 3
My Story. 5
Labyrinthitis 10
Symptoms. 11
Other Types of Inner Ear Disorders 12
List of More Symptoms of an Inner Ear Disorder 13
Getting a Diagnosis and the Different Tests 14
Treatment. 18
Balance Therapy and Vestibular Rehabilitation. 20
What to Eat, and Not to Eat? That is the Question. 22
Vincent Van Gogh 23
Feeling Good Again 25
    Journalize
    Affirm!
    Vent!
    Keep a positive attitude
    Set Goals! And, Keep Dreaming
    Get on the Internet…Go to the Library!
    Spend time with family and friends
    Be thankful
    Create a Survival Kit

My Journal	31
Poem	37
Places that help…	38
References	41

Acknowledgements

First I would like to thank the Creator, God my father, for all of his blessings and for the strength he has given me to make it through all tough times. I thank HIM for everything! I want to thank my husband, Lonnie, Jr. for loving me unconditionally, supporting me and standing behind me in all of my endeavors. Thank you for taking care of me! Thank you for putting up with me when I get into my moods. You are my first and only love. My children, Jada and Lonnie, III…I love you two so much. You two keep me going, even when I don't always feel like it. You two are the best babies in the world! My mommy, Judi, thank you for listening to my ideas, problems, frustrations, and everything else you have done for me in this life. You are the heart of my support system. My daddy, Linwood, who I get a lot of my qualities from, but I don't think he believes it. To my sister, Buffy, for your love and advice. My brother, Tristan, for everything you are. I thank both of you for making me laugh all of the time. And, my nephew Will, who is a great basketball player and will make it big someday as long as he does well in school! My second mother, Pam, who has remained strong in the toughest of all times. To all of my brothers and sisters-in-law…Cynthia, Londell, Lontrell, Lonnell, Lonrae and Lonise. I love you all. My friends Salwa, Dorian, Leslie, Donna, Takiyah, Daily, Billy (Hendrix), Tyia, and Kandace. And, to those who aren't physically with us anymore, but are spiritually…My uncle John (Bam-Bam), my father-in-law, Lonnie, Sr. and my Grammy and Grampy Sandstrom. May you all Rest In Peace. And, to everyone else who loves me. I love you all, too.

Introduction

Imagine not having your balance. Imagine feeling like you are going to tip over every minute of every day. Can you imagine waking up one day and you can't brush your hair, or teeth without having a hard time? Because when you tilt your head just slightly...it feels like you are going to fall down. Imagine not being able to take a walk without the fear of falling. Or, go to a doctor appointment and can't sit in the waiting room because the person sitting next to you keeps moving and it's making you feel like you are on a boat during a storm. Imagine that the once, soft living room carpet that you loved to sink your feet in, now makes you feel like you are standing on a waterbed. Can you imagine that the once familiar walk, although in the dark, to the bathroom in the middle of the night, can no longer be walked? Can you imagine being afraid to drive? Or, what if you couldn't rest on your couch and watch a television show without feeling dizzy from the cushion and the movements on the television screen. Can you imagine that? Could you really? If you have never suffered from an inner ear disorder personally...I doubt that you can.

When I first got sick with labyrinthitis, a type of inner ear infection, I did not know that it would change my life forever. I just thought it was a virus that would go away and I would never think of it again. But, the virus, itself did go away but now I suffer with the damage it caused to my inner ear and balance system.

When I first came down with labyrinthitis, of course, just like the majority of people, I had never heard of it before. So, I asked questions to my doctor and Ear, Nose and Throat Specialist. And, all I ever got was, "You'll get better...it just takes time." So I had to do a great deal of research on my own.

Most doctors have very little experience with inner ear disorders and the balance system. Inner ear problems also don't get the attention that they should. There is not enough awareness and education on this disorder. I think it's because the virus is invisible to everyone, but the sufferer. The sufferer looks and appears to be normal and healthy. Sufferers are also very misunderstood. Friends, family members, co-workers and even doctors may think we are suffering from some type of psychological problem, which is totally untrue. This disorder is very real. It's not something that is just "all in the person's mind."

I have written this book for my fellow "dizzies" (that's anyone who has suffered from an inner ear disorder that has caused them to experience dizziness) and their loved ones. I hope that through the words on the following pages I will be able to provide all of the information I can about inner ear disorders, especially labyrinthitis. I hope that by sharing my experiences as a patient and sufferer of this disorder, I can help other sufferers to stay strong.

Please note, that I am not a doctor, or a health professional. I am only a patient and sufferer of this disorder. This book is about my experiences and my own research. It is not intended to be used as a source of diagnosis and treatment. If you need health advice, or have concerns about your well being, contact your health professional.

Balance as a Sixth Sense

We all learn about our five senses and what they are in elementary or grade school as a child. We learn that they are see, touch, hear, feel and taste. But, no one taught us that there is also one very important, often unnoticed sense. That is our vestibular system, our sense of balance.

I never thought about my balance. I never thought about standing up straight, or sitting on a bed. I didn't think about all of the mechanisms in my inner ear and brain that controlled my sense of direction, the way I saw the world. It was natural. None of this crossed my mind, until I lost mine.

The sense of balance is controlled by our inner ears. Our inner ears send information to our brain about our direction, whether we are lying down, or standing up. Whether we are turning around, looking up. Our inner ears coordinate our movements. And, it is our sensory processor, in which tunes and fine-tunes all sensory information entering the brain. Every thing you see, light…dark. The sounds that you hear, motions you feel, gravity, temperature, humidity and barometric pressure are all fine-tuned by the mechanisms in the inner ear and then it's sent to our brain. The inner ear also controls our motor skills. It coordinates our eyes, head, hands, fingers, feet, and toes. The proprioceptive system is also a part of the vestibular system; this is where special receptors in our muscles and joints send information to our brain. As you can see our vestibular and balance system is very complex.

It is said that our vestibular system has the most important influence on all other senses and our quality of life. So, I wonder why it isn't included with the other five senses?

When our balance system is damaged, it has little ability to repair itself. Because of damage to one or both ears, mixed signals or unmatched signals are sent to the brain. The way we recover from a balance injury is called "compensation." Compensation is the process in which our brain recalibrates itself. This usually occurs naturally in most people through time and movement. For others, they may require vestibular therapy.

Then, you have "decompensation", or "setbacks." Decompensation means that somewhere during the recovery process from an inner ear disorder, the brain forgot the fine-tuning that it created in the beginning phase of recovery. Decompensation can happen when you catch a cold, or the flu. It can happen when you take a vacation, get pregnant, or have surgery. Decompensation can happen when you do anything that you don't normally do. For example, if you normally work a 40-hour workweek, then work 20 hours of overtime…It can cause decompensation. But, the good thing is that recovery from decompensation is much quicker than the initial compensation process.

Preventing Balance Problems…

Some things you can do to prevent ever having a balance problem are:

1. Never EVER put a q-tip, bobby pin or anything into your ear. I used to clean my ears with a q-tip all of the time. This is not a good thing at all to do. Doctors will tell you to never put anything in your ear smaller than your elbow.
2. If you ever get an ear infection, or have pain or itchiness in your ear, consult a doctor.
3. Avoid very loud noises.
4. Never hold in a sneeze. The pressure could damage you ear.

Your balance can also be damaged by…

A viral infection, or bacterial infection. Things like the flu, sinusitis, swimmer's ear, a sore throat, and trauma to the head (have you ever seen a boxer get hit really hard and they become dizzy?) or trauma to the brain can also result in damage to your inner ear. Fluid build-up in the ear, rarely tumors, and even, allergies could cause problems. My dizziness and imbalance began after I had sinusitis.

My Story

This is my story about labyrinthitis, an invisible, but debilitating inner ear disorder. Please remember, I am not a medical doctor and this book is not a source of medical diagnosis. This is a story of my experiences only and my research on this disorder.

It was August of 2002; we had just relocated to Hampton, Virginia, from Ellsworth Air Force Base, South Dakota. The year, so far, had been hectic and full of change. I left employment at a great place where I worked as a computer technician. I was still in college and had just had a baby girl, Jada. After her birth, I was experiencing migraine headaches and mild postpartum depression. I must say I was really stressed. But, I just knew things would get better when my family and I got back home to the East Coast. (I'm originally from Washington, D.C. Hampton, VA is just three hours away.) I figured everything would be great once I returned home and was around the rest of our family. I hadn't been close to my family in five years because of my earlier military career. I was looking forward to my new life.

My husband, Lonnie and I bought our first house in Hampton. I was so excited…my very own house on a cul-de-sac, with a walk in closet, huge backyard and fireplace! I was just so ecstatic. Everything was going great. Then, I got sick…

It began in October of 2002. Well, looking back…hindsight is 20/20…in September a couple of days after my 24th birthday; I experienced a strange dizziness in my sleep. I woke up frightened…holding on to dear life, screaming, "Help me!" I thought maybe I partied too much for my birthday, drinking and it was catching up with me. Then about a week later…I experienced sinus headaches and nasal drip. So I went to my family practice doctor and was prescribed Augmentin for sinusitis.

I began my medication and then a week later, my husband and I were driving home from furniture shopping and while sitting at a red traffic light…I heard a strange buzzing in my right ear, and then brief dizziness again. Okay, so I thought…I wondered what it was. But, I just thought it had something to do with my sinuses. So, I ignored it.

It was about my eighth day on Augmentin and three days after the buzzing in my ear at that red traffic light. I remember it clearly; it was October 3, 2002. I woke up early that morning, with the world spinning (or me) out of control. I was so terrified. I called my doctor's office to let them know what was going on. I wanted to know if it was possible that I could be having an allergic reaction to the antibiotics. The nurse said, "No." There were no appointments available to be seen that day, so I went in to the emergency room at the hospital.

At the ER I sat in the waiting room, feeling lopsided and dizzy. I had a million thoughts a minute running through my mind. I didn't want anything to be terribly wrong with me.

"I didn't want to die."

"What about Jada? I want to watch her grow up?"

"What about Jr.? What will he do?"

"Gillian Barnett." A nurse called for me and separated me from my thoughts.

I stood up and almost fell to the floor. The swirling in my head would not stop. It felt like my head was on a malfunctioning merry-go-round, spinning…fast…faster, not slowing down. I had to have the nurse help me walk to the treatment room.

I sat on the table…I remember closing my eyes to relieve the swirling and twirling of my brain but it didn't help. I just sat there holding on to dear life, scared and confused. Mostly scared.

The emergency room doctor came in and asked me for the symptoms that I was experiencing. I told him that I was just extremely dizzy. He then checked my eyes and ears.

He diagnosed me with Otitis Media—a middle ear infection. He said there was fluid on my ears, which was causing the imbalance and dizziness. Once again, I was back on Augmentin and now a prescription of Meclizine (a medicine for nausea and dizziness.) I was told to follow up with my family practice doctor in a week.

A week went by and I was sitting in the waiting room. This time I was at the family practice doctor. My nerves were so bad. I was sitting there and I was sure that I was sitting up straight, but it felt like I was tilting to the right. I was watching people who looked normal and wish it were me. I didn't understand what was going on with me. These were strange symptoms and I didn't think that an ear could cause so many problems.

Once I was called back to the treatment room, the family practice doctor asked me for my symptoms. I told him that I was dizzy, that I felt like I was tilting to the side and felt lopsided.

"Have you ever seen one of those old V8 vegetable drink commercials and the person is walking lopsided because they didn't have their V8 drink?" That's how I felt. I only wish a simple drink would have been my cure.

The doctor checked my ears and my eyes. He also said there was a little fluid on my right ear. He then performed the Dix-Hallpike exam to look for a nystagmus, a characteristic movement of the eyes. In this test, the patient is seated on the table. The doctor then lowers the patient's head to the table and turns the head to one side. The doctor then watches the patient's eyes for the nystagmus. If the patient gets dizzy and exhibits nystagmus, the ear pointed to the floor is the affected ear. If nystagmus is not seen, the doctor will repeat the test on the other side, checking the other ear. I don't think he found one with me. So, he then referred me to an Ear, Nose and Throat specialist.

My appointment with the Ear, Nose and Throat specialist wasn't for another two weeks. "Gosh! I was so disappointed! Do these people understand what it's like to feel dizzy and imbalanced non-stop?" This was a real emergency to me! But it didn't seem to be a big deal to the doctor's or anyone else around. I felt so alone.

The Ear, Nose and Throat doctor was really optimistic about my recovery. He made me feel so comfortable and assured me that what I had was called labyrinthitis.

"Lab-ee...what?" I thought. (Lab-ee-ren-thi-tis) It is a dysfunction of the inner ear. The labyrinth is a fluid filled semi-circular organ in the ear. When it becomes inflamed as a result of a bacteria or viral infection, it can cause hearing and balance problems. My labyrinthitis came from a viral infection. It came right after the sinus infection that I had. The ENT doctor told me it could last from six to eight weeks.

When my eight-week mark approached it was the New Year, January 2003. I was starting to feel "somewhat" better. I definitely wasn't 100%. I finally decided to start exercising again and try to lose all the excess weight I had gained while pregnant the past year and while sick. I don't know what I was thinking when I made part of my exercise regimen to jump rope. BAD IDEA! I jumped rope and my vertigo and dizziness came back just as it had when this entire thing first started. Full-blown vertigo all over again! The jump rope caused too much impact to my ear. Mild and moderate exercise is best when you are recovering from labyrinthitis. I wasn't fully aware of this at first. I had to learn the hard way.

I became really depressed...I was crying all of the time and feeling sorry for myself. I felt beat up and I did not feel like my old self at all. I felt like I had died and was now living as someone else. This someone else felt like a zombie...I felt like I was on drugs, or drunk. I had a baby to take care of, to play with. I had a husband who was working and coming home taking care of me. I became very dependent on him. I never wanted to be away from him. I needed to be around him at all times. He made me feel secure. I just wanted him there just in case I needed him during one of my dizzy spells. I never wanted him to leave. I became really needy and insecure. This was so unlike me. All of this fostered and kept feeding my depression. The once independent person was gone. I used to work everyday—even when I was sick. I remember the days when I would go shopping, to the malls, walking around Wal-Mart alone…having one of my great days. I remember going to the clubs, out to eat with friends…Now, I wouldn't step foot out of the front door without my hubby by my side. I missed the old me.

I also became mean. I didn't seem to care about anyone's feelings. Not that I wanted to be like this—it was just that I had my ear on my mind 24/7. This sickness corrupts your life…it interrupts it to the point where you can't ignore it. Some things you can ignore, like a scratch on your arm, or a slight headache. You can still walk around and feel normal with a sore arm. But, you can't with an inner ear disorder like labyrinthitis. I became so irritated, that I began taking it out on my poor husband. I would pick arguments with him for small stupid things. So stupid that I cannot remember any of the reasons to even give an example.

It was more than the eight weeks that the doctor told me it takes for this "head monster" to go away. So, now anxiety and worry set in. I now believed I had a brain tumor. I felt that I was going to die of this and was worried and anxious all of the time. I practically begged my family practice doctor for a referral for an MRI. And, even though he didn't think I needed one, he ordered the MRI for me. I didn't know that I was claustrophobic before this procedure. Or, maybe the procedure itself made me this way. But, anyway, after waiting two weeks, the results came back normal. Thank God for that!

My anxiousness went away after my MRI results came back normal. At least I knew there was nothing wrong with my brain. But, the imbalance and dizziness was still there.

I began rating my life and well being on a percentage scale. With normalcy being 100%, I was feeling 86%-90% most of the time. This was between the months of March 2003 and September 2003.

By the time Thanksgiving 2003 rolled around…I had been plagued with this labyrinthitis for 13 months. I began feeling about 96%-99%. Never really 100%. And, if I did feel 100%, I didn't really notice. But, when I did get to 100%, and dropped to a 99%, boy did I notice the difference. But at least now I believed I was healing...finally.

It is the present and I have had the after effects for 21 months now. But, I do feel 100% most of the time. When I drop down on the percentage scale...I really can tell and it upsets me. But, I keep moving. I noticed that when it's humid, or when it's expected to rain, I feel a bit off. There was something my nephew, Will, told me a while back when I was upset.

"Aunt Jill, maybe it's a blessing to have that ear problem..."

"You're special," he said. "You will always know ahead of time, when it will rain."

I thought that was so sweet. I still think about that when it rains or when I feel it will rain.

I realize and understand how hard I had made it for my husband. He's in the military, working full-time. But he still managed to come home and (on my "starry nights") cook dinner. Not only would he cook the dinner, but also he would fix my plate and bring it to me. He would also clean the house, wash clothes and go grocery shopping. He did everything except for bathe me. He got stressed, I know. But, it was and sometimes, still so hard for me. I hate feeling like this and wish to be fully independent again. I don't know what I would have ever done without his love and support. I did manage to take care of my daughter and read to her and play with her. But, it was a chore.

Now, I have a two and a half month son, Lonnie, III. My pregnancy with him didn't affect my compensation that much. I was lucky. I still have some "off" days. When it is humid outside, raining...I feel different, just a tad bit "off". When I'm tired, or if I sleep too much...I also feel a little off balance. But, I have gotten better.

Having this disorder has taught me a lot. I've learned to appreciate my health, my life and my family more than ever. That's one reason why I wrote this book. I've always wanted to write and this sickness gave me that beginning. It has given me the EXPERIENCE, the knowledge, the strength and the courage to pursue my dreams as a writer. I only hope this book helps and comforts those with this "invisible" sickness. I want my dizzy friends to know that it really does get better. Only time can heal this, just have faith. It'll happen.

Labyrinthitis

What is labyrinthitis?

The labyrinth is one of our organs that not only contributes to our hearing, but also helps to control our balance. The labyrinth is the semi-circular organ in the inner ear that is filled with fluid.

There are also tiny hair cells in there that all work together. The labyrinth is a very small organ in which, if it does get a virus—it's so small and filled with fluid that it makes it hard for it to come out. You know, it's almost like getting a sore in you mouth—it takes longer to heal because it's always warm and wet in your mouth. Well, at least your mouth gets some air when you open and close it, so it helps the sore to heal. Your labyrinth doesn't get any air.

Labyrinthitis is the name given to the labyrinth when it becomes inflamed, or infected. It can be a result of a viral or bacterial infection. The viral infection is the most common. And, because those semi-circular canals and nerves are so sensitive, after a viral infection such as labyrinthitis, or trauma…we can be left dizzy for a very long time. I've read that the damage could sometimes be permanent, but the symptoms, most often aren't…because of compensation.

The nerves and hair cells of the labyrinth also tend to degenerate as we approach old age…this is why some people experience hearing loss, brief periods of dizziness and a feeling of being off-balanced and unsteady when they get older.

Symptoms

The most common symptom of labyrinthitis is vertigo. Vertigo is the sensation of movement; it can be spinning or whirling. Vertigo caused by labyrinthitis begins suddenly. It can start at any time, most of the time, without warning. It can be from moderate to severe enough that it leads to vomiting and nausea. I personally did not have problems with vomiting, but I did have nausea a great deal in the beginning of my dizzy experience.

I've read during my research on this disorder, that it can last from a couple of days to weeks…. From my experience, and those of others I know from the health boards that are suffering from this disorder…this is not always the case. The majority of people suffer from weeks to months. Sometimes, even years.

I remember being very upset because my sickness was lasting for so long. I didn't believe I only had a viral infection, because of what I read, said I would only be sick for a couple of days. And, now I still have some symptoms and it is two years later.

Other symptoms of labyrinthitis, or lab (what I like to call it) include tinnitus, which is a ringing or buzzing sound in the ears, or you can have some hearing loss, and a feeling of imbalance. Imbalance usually comes later, after the spinning is gone. (In some cases, the imbalance can begin without the spinning.)

Depression and anxiety can also result from this disorder. Labyrinthitis can leave the sufferer feeling lonely, helpless and uptight. Worriness and stress can also take hold.

I knew that no one really understood what I was going through, or how I felt because I "seemed" and "appeared" to be healthy and normal. No one could actually see my sickness. This is tough to deal with, because no one really knows what you are dealing with while sick with this disorder. Doctors that have never had lab don't even know how it feels. Unless you have suffered from labyrinthitis, there is no way you can tell someone how they are feeling. The real "experts" on this disorder, are those who have been through it themselves.

Other Types of Inner Ear Disorders

Meniere's Disease is a disorder of the fluid balance mechanism in the inner ear. There is no cure for this disorder. Symptoms include, loud ringing in the ears, or buzzing, dizziness, and nausea. This disease is what some researchers believe Vincent Van Gogh suffered from.

Benign Positional Vertigo (BPPV) results from damage to the delicate sensory units of the balance portion of the inner ear. Damage can occur after labyrinthitis. Symptoms include spinning and lightheadedness when the head changes certain positions. Nausea may result from the spinning, but there is no hearing loss, or tinnitus with BPPV. The Epley maneuver can help with this disorder. If you have BPPV, your doctor has probably already told you about this.

Perilymph Fistula can occur after a sudden change in barometric pressure. Changes include pressure in the air during airplane travel, scuba diving or a major head injury. (Boxers can experience this after blows to their head.) The change in pressure can cause a rupture in one of the membranes that separate the middle ear from the inner ear. This allows the inner ear fluid to escape into the middle ear. Symptoms of perilymph fistula include hearing loss or tinnitus, vertigo or lightheadedness, and ear pressure.

Acoustic Neuroma is a benign tumor that grows on the balance nerve. Vertigo is not usually experienced with acoustic neuroma, but tinnitus and hearing loss are the main symptoms. The tumor must be surgically removed.

List of More Symptoms of an Inner Ear Disorder

Lightheadness
Giddiness
Spinning, or whirling sensation, vertigo
Swimming sensation
Wooziness
Unsteadiness
Jumpy vision
Feeling of bouncing when walking
Motion sickness/Car sickness
Dysequilibrium
Nausea
Vomiting
Ringing, or buzzing in the ears
Ear drainage
Earache
Itchiness of the ear
Neck soreness
Headache
Dizziness is made worse at movies, or cinemas
Difficulty sleeping, and getting into a position that stops the dizziness

Getting a Diagnosis and the Different Tests

According to the National Institutes of Health, nearly half the people in the United States will seek help for dizziness or poor balance sometime in their lives. Vertigo and dizziness can be a result of many disorders, but most of the time it is because of the inner ear.

The doctor will go over your medical history and probably ask you if you are on any medications. This is to rule out any vertigo, or dizziness that can result from drug interactions, or any other health problems. (Other health problems can include, heart problems, high blood pressure, etcetera.) (If the doctor doesn't ask about medications you may be on—tell him, or her.)

He or she will then give you a physical examination, which may include the Dix-Hallpike exam also called the Nylen-Barany test. During this exam, you will be asked to sit with your legs extended on the exam table. The doctor will then turn your head 45º toward one side and will help you to quickly lie back so your head hangs over the end of the table. The doctor will watch your eyes to see if your eyes jump, or have a nystagmus. The timing and appearance of your eye movements will help your doctor to tell if your vertigo is inner ear or in your central nervous system.

After you sit back up for a few minutes to recover from the vertigo, the doctor will repeat the procedure in the opposite direction. Note that a nystagmus can't always be found with this procedure. My doctor didn't find one with me.

The Dix-Hallpike is done to help identify the location of the problem that is causing vertigo, such as the inner ear or the central nervous system. If the problem is in the ear, it can determine which ear is affected.

Your exam will also include the doctor looking into your ears for signs of an ear infection. This can also determine which ear is the problem ear.

If the cause of your vertigo is not clear from the medical history and physical examination, your doctor may want to refer you to a specialist such as an otolaryngologist or neuro-otologist or otoneurologist for vestibular testing and to do more tests, such as a neurological exam. These tests will help the doctor to determine if the problem is in the inner ear, the brain, or the nerves of the central nervous system.

Other than the Dix-Hallpike exam, the different tests that may be given also include the following:

Of course, the otoscope exam—Everyone should know what an otoscope is. It's the small device that doctors use to look into your ears. It shines a small beam of light inside the ear. This helps the doctor to look for signs of an ear infection and to look at your eardrum. This is probably the first test you will get when you complain of an ear problem, or the dizzies.

Moving Platform Posturography (MVP)—This test quantifies balance and the vestibular function. It helps specialists to be able to tell if your balance is improving or not. This test is administered by strapping you on to parachute-type equipment and then you will step onto a platform, which will then move. The machine will record all of your actions and create a record for the doctor to review.

Rotational chair testing—This test involves rotating in a chair in a darkened booth while your eye position, the nystagmus, is monitored. There are three parts to this test. They include: the chair test, the optokinetic test, and the fixation test. The dizzy patient actually becomes less dizzy during this test.

Vestibular Auto-Rotation Test (VAT)—I have read that this is the most accurate and easiest balance test to perform of all diagnostic balance tests available today. The VAT records and analyzes the performance of the inner ear.

Epley Maneuver—The maneuver starts sitting upright. This maneuver should be done by your doctor or physical therapist both for safety (you may be dizzy) and to observe the eye movements.

First, your doctor will have you briskly lie on your back with your head turned to the symptomatic side at a 45-degree angle. Your head will be kept in this position for 30 to 60 seconds, based on the duration of the vertigo as measured by observation of your eye movements (the nystagmus). You will probably be dizzy for the first 10 seconds.

Next your doctor will turn your head to the other side, and keep it in that position for another 30 to 60 seconds. You might get dizzy again.

Audiogram—This is the basic hearing test. You know, like the ones you get when you enter school? An audiologist will administer this test. The audiogram tests the ability to hear pure tones.

You will be seated in a sound proof room while the audiologist goes next door and administers the test. I have had many of these tests just to make sure that my hearing improved after an ear infection, or sometimes just to make sure I had no hearing loss during my battle with labyrinthitis.

This test takes about five to ten minutes. The test includes the audiologist asking you to repeat different words after them at different levels. And, to raise your hand when you hear tones. For instance, if you hear a sound in your left ear, you will raise your left hand.

A complete audiogram will test both the bone conduction (the ability to hear a sound when it transmitted through bone) and the air conduction (the ability to hear a sound when it transmitted through air). A comparison between these two types of conduction can be very useful in localizing which part of the hearing mechanism is responsible for the loss. The audiogram test is useful in determining if the loss is due to a problems with the portion of the middle ear that conducts sound from the ear canal to the inner ear (in which case it would be called a "conductive" hearing loss) or if it is due to the inner ear or the nerve that conducts the sound signals to the brain (in which case it would be called a "sensorineural" hearing loss). The sensoineural hearing loss is sometimes experienced with labyrinthitis.

Tympanogram (tim-pah-noh-gram)—The tympanogram measures the pressure in the ear. A special probe that looks something like an earplug is placed up to the ear canal and then it measures the pressure. You should not talk, swallow or move during the test because all of these can affect the measurement. And, you want your test results to be accurate. So it's important to just be still. I never had this test, but I probably would giggle, or swallow, or something just because they say that you shouldn't.

The tympanogram will tell the provider if there is any fluid in your middle ear, or if there is any earwax impacted way down in the canal. (I get this problem in my right "bad" ear at times, and my ENT has to professionally clean it out.) The tympanogram can also tell of problems with the eardrum, such as scarring or a perforation, or a tumor in the middle ear. This simple test as you can see, can reveal many different things.

Auditory Brain Stem Response or ABR—The ABR is a special hearing test that can be used to track the nerve signals arising in the inner ear as they travel through the hearing nerve (called the auditory nerve) to the region of the brain responsible for hearing. The test is useful because it can tell the provider where along that path the hearing loss has occurred. For example, the ABR is often used for individuals with a sensorineural (nerve) loss in just one ear. This loss can sometimes be caused by a benign (non-cancerous) tumor on the auditory nerve.

If the ABR is normal along that region of the path, the chances of having this tumor are quite small.

The ABR can also be used on small infants since it requires no conscious response from the person being tested. A small speaker is placed near the ear, which produces clicking sound. Special electrodes automatically record the nerve signal; the patient can even be asleep during the test.

Electronystagmogram or ENG—The ENG is a special test of the balance mechanism of the inner ear. The test involves running a cool liquid in the ear and then a warm liquid. This is called the caloric test. The water is run through a small tube that is placed in the ear canal. This change in temperature stimulates the inner ear, which in turn causes rapid reflex movements of the eyes. There are also three more parts to this test, they include: the calibration test which evaluates rapid movements of the eyes, the positional test, which measures dizziness from different positions of the head, and the tracking test that evaluates the eyes as it looks at a target. These movements reflect how well the balance mechanism is working.

Electrocochleography or ECoG—ECoG is a test that examines the electrical potentials of the inner ear. This can determine if there is excess fluid pressure that can cause problems with hearing and dizziness.

Magnetic Resonance Imaging or MRI—MRI studies have a limited role for evaluation of dizziness and imbalance and it's usually considered only after a comprehensive evaluation has been completed or when there are specific symptoms and signs that suggest focal neurologic problems. Sometimes, your doctor will order this test to relieve any anxieties stemmed from being sick for so long. If you doctor doesn't think you need a MRI, then you probably don't. But, it's always best to trust your instincts. If you want one done, then it is your right. I felt so much better mentally, knowing that I did not have a brain tumor.

Treatment

The best treatment for recovering from labyrinthitis is movement. YOU MUST MOVE! I know this is hard to do, but it is a must. After the first week of labyrinthitis, it is important to get out and move. No matter how you are feeling. MOVE! Start off slow with short walks. The visual stimulation during walks is good for the brain in order to compensate.

It's important also, not to overdo it. Jogging, running, jumping rope, or lifting heavy weights could make things worse in the early weeks of lab. I'm sure this is the same for other inner ear disorders.

With lab, it is difficult to do everyday chores, such as cleaning, washing the dishes, or vacuuming. But, keep doing these things. Don't let others do it for you. The brain has to relearn everything in order to compensate. After letting my husband do everything for a while, I realized that if I were to have kept of doing daily chores, I probably would have felt better much quicker than I did.

Driving is also very difficult and I don't recommend it until you can walk without feeling imbalanced. But, once that imbalanced sensation resolves, go for a short drive around your neighborhood with a family member or friend who can take over the wheel if you become overwhelmed. Your brain will have to take this all in…the visual stimulation may make you feel off, but you will be improving. Also, from my experience, just to let you know…when it rains, you will probably use window shield wipers…this can make you feel very dizzy if you are still in the early stages of the compensation phase.

When you try to do things and feel bad afterwards, don't fret…it's just your brain fine-tuning itself. You actually will feel "off" every time your brain compensates for something new. And, I say new because that's what it's like now that you have to recompensate.

Balance therapy and vestibular rehabilitation, also know VRT are also forms to treating balance and dizziness disorders. I'll explain these a little more in detail in the next chapter.

During the first episodes of vertigo, your doctor may give you some medications to help relieve the symptoms, such as Meclizine or Anti-vert and Benadryl. Or, sedatives such as Valium may be prescribed. I do not recommend using these vestibular suppressants. This is just my advice—I am not a doctor. But, if you feel you must, then go right ahead; just don't use them for more than one week. I say this because these types of medications slow the compensation process down. I didn't use them at all and my compensation has taken a while, so I can only imagine how long it would have taken if I were to use these medications.

If you suffer long-term from lab, you may become depressed, or suffer from anxiety. If you are feeling sad, anxious, not eating or have any feelings of suicide please contact your physician right away. I became very depressed and had to take prescription anti-depressants. It's okay to get help when you need it.

Balance Therapy and Vestibular Rehabilitation

Studies show that 85 percent of people with inner-ear problems get at least partial relief from vestibular rehabilitation, and 30 percent recover completely.

As I stated earlier, balance is a very complicated function. And, if you have suffered, or are currently suffering from a balance disorder such as labyrinthitis…then you know how complicated it is with first-hand experience.

Vestibular therapy is based on the concept that the very movements that make the patient dizzy can eventually relieve the symptoms through repetition. By repeatedly bombarding the brain with the incorrect messages, the brain is ultimately forced to adapt, accepting and reinterpreting the faulty signals as correct. When that happens, the symptoms subside. This is called "compensation."

Balance therapy and vestibular exercises are usually custom designed home-exercise programs, which includes habituation exercises, like neck and leg exercises and gentle movement exercises. These activities are very simple routines that can be done many times during the day.

Along with habituation exercises, patients are given eye exercises that retrain the eye reflexes. Adjustments in the eye reflexes are controlled by the inner ear and allow the eye to keep the field of vision steady as a person moves. In one of the eye exercises, patients repeatedly move their heads from side to side or up and down while focusing on a specific target, like a picture on the wall. This helps the patient to steady their gaze.

Patients also do balance retraining exercises, which force the brain to rely on information from the inner ear rather than messages from the eyes and the feet.

In the vast majority of cases of chronic balance disorders, the physical damage in the inner ear is permanent, but the dizziness does not have to be permanent because of the compensation mechanisms.

Associated problems with concentration, memory loss, fatigue, and depression can often accompany inner-ear problems. I did not know this at first. I noticed that my memory wasn't as sharp as it used to be. And, I was having a hard time concentrating on my college work. These problems develop because the brain is working so hard simply to keep the body upright, that other brain functions are compromised. These symptoms may naturally disappear along with the dizziness. What a complex body we have!

Most inner-ear disorders require anywhere from four to six weeks of physical therapy, with exercises performed two to five times a day at home and once or twice a week in therapy sessions. The program is constantly revised as the patient improves. The exercises must be carefully monitored by a physical therapist because too much activity too soon can be counterproductive.

Vestibular rehabilitation is not for everyone. Some more serious inner-ear disorders require medication or surgery. However, doctors and practitioners say the success rate of this drug-free, risk-free treatment has made it one of the fastest-growing areas of physical therapy.

What to Eat, and Not to Eat? That is the Question.

A diet that is low in salt is beneficial to those with inner ear disorders. Caffeine should be limited too, or avoided. I went from drinking sodas with caffeine to those with no caffeine. And, I don't eat as much chocolate anymore. (I can't totally stop eating chocolate, though!) This not only helps my symptoms of labyrinthitis, but it's also helping me to eat healthier.

I am not a big coffee drinker and I don't drink alcohol, except occasionally like for birthdays. (But, I haven't even sipped alcohol since I came down with labyrinthitis.) Alcohol can already make you feel woozy and off. So, it's best to limit the intake of caffeine and alcohol, or just stay away from them.

It is important to follow a healthy diet rich in fruits and vegetables. This is not only important just because you are sick, but it's important for maintaining your health. Period. I went from eating at all times of the day. If I was busy, I would skip meals, eat fast food, and a lot of sweets. My diet was probably a big cause to me falling ill from this horrible inner ear virus in the first place. My immune system wasn't strong enough.

I began taking vitamins and drinking a lot of water. I didn't drink much water before I was diagnosed with labyrinthitis, either. Water is so good for you. It helps you to not retain water in your body, which could possibly make your ear symptoms act up. It may even improve them, as it did for me. Water cleanses your system of toxins that can make you sick. Water keeps me energized and I love what it has done for my skin. I feel and look so much healthier because of water. If you don't like water, all I can tell you is—"TO GET OVER IT!" Add, a slice of lemon to your water for a light taste. Believe me…you'll feel better.

As for medications…

When you are taking any type of medications, always check the side effects. Sometimes medications cause dizziness and drowsiness that can make your problem worse. Sometimes, there are alternative medications that you could possibly take. This is a good thing to discuss with your doctor.

Vincent Van Gogh

Most people know of the famous Dutch painter, Vincent van Gogh. Some of his famous works include, "Sunflowers," "Pavement Café' at Night" and "Starry Night" which is ironically my favorite piece of art. I say this because Van Gogh's painting of the bright stars in the sky at night depicted the way he felt on the inside. He created this painting in an asylum where he was being treated for insanity.

"Starry Night" was his depiction of the vertigo he was experiencing. Yes, Van Gogh suffered from an inner ear disorder. I do not believe he was crazy, or insane. And, if he was, it was only after his inner ear disorder drove him to be that way.

Some researchers think he may have suffered from Meniere's disease. Meniere's disease is an inner ear disorder that causes the sufferer to have bouts of vertigo, nausea and loud ringing in one, or both of the ears. No one really knows how this develops and there is no cure. Some say Van Gogh went crazy when he realized he couldn't be cured. This was back in the 1800's. At least now in this day in age, we have the technology, resources and knowledge to at least relieve the symptoms.

As a result of his "insanity," Van Gogh cut his left ear off. I totally understand the feeling behind his self-mutilation. There are plenty of times when I would be crying, or so angry at my ear that I would just scream, "I wish I could cut my damn ear off!" That's how bad I would feel. So, I sympathize with the famous painter. It's sad that he had to deal with this inner ear disorder, let alone having to deal with people saying he was suffering from paranoia and delusions. I do believe he was depressed, but I do not believe the poor guy was crazy.

In letters from Van Gogh written to his brother, Theo, he tells of the ringing in his ears, his nausea and his violent dizzy episodes. The "dizzy episodes" is what makes people believe he had Meniere's disease.

From other stories I have read, they say Van Gogh was depressed because he could not find love and his paintings weren't selling well. Perhaps he was saddened because of that. But, he wasn't crazy; and that's just what I think.

I don't believe the poor guy was just "hearing things." In my opinion, that was tinnitus. (Remember, tinnitus is the ringing, or buzzing in the ears.)

After experiencing an inner ear disorder, I definitely understand why Van Gogh became depressed, withdrawn and cut his ear lobe off.

Feeling Good Again

I can assure you that you will feel good again. It will take some people longer than others to recover. We all have different bodies. I have "get-well" advice that has helped me immensely through this tough time. I have included it in this book in hopes that it will help you, too.

*Journalize...*just as I did.

Write down your thoughts, fears, anxieties, and progress. Some things to include...the weather, activities you participated in, such a mowing the grass, reading while laying on your side, going to the movies. Write down the things you have eaten. How do you feel on a particular day? Rate your wellness on a scale. As I said earlier, I would rate myself on a percentage scale with 100% the best.

Journalizing helps you to keep track of your progress. Your journal will show you how you actually improve when you don't notice it yourself. The journal is a good way to vent. It is also a good source to help you come up with questions for your doctor. Or, you can let friends and family members read it to help them gain a better understanding of your ailment.

"Fear of the pain blinds us to the goal of HEALING. Only by seeing our problems clearly and experiencing them can we do something about them."
—*Bob Hoffman, American Peak Performance Consultant, Author*

Affirm!

Write down daily affirmations such as, "I'm going to have a great day!" Or, "I feel good today!" "I'm healthy, I'm alive!" And, say them as many times as you can throughout the day.

Say them to yourself in the mirror when you brush your teeth in the morning. Train your subconscious mind as to how you want and know you should feel. I recommend saying your affirmations at least twenty times a day. Not only say them, but also believe them!

<u>*Affirmations*</u>
"I love me!"
"I am happy!"
"I have so many good things in life to focus on."
"There is nothing to worry about, I'll be fine."

Vent! *(A few minutes a day)*
Don't just sit around and feel sorry for yourself. I did this for a while and finally got over it. I know you need to grieve because your life feels different and dizzy. Losing your balance is a major change. You will grieve because of your loss of your balance. But, grieving is good for the soul. Going through a major life alteration such as labyrinthitis takes a great deal from you. You will go through a period where you just can't believe this has happened to you. And you will get angry and mad. You'll be sad and confused at times. And, I know that most of the time you don't feel good because of all of the emotional roller coasters. So do what I do…I set aside five to ten minutes to be angry, or sad everyday. (Or, to experience any of these emotions.) If you need to cry…cry. If you need to punch a pillow…punch it. But, don't allow grief and sadness to occupy your entire day. After those five to ten minutes—let it go and move on with your day. Stress only makes this thing worse; it could even make you sicker. So, experience all of the emotions that you need to in order to patch up your soul. But only give it a limited time each day. Because, "You have so much MORE to live for!"

Keep a positive attitude… A positive attitude makes all the difference. Take this experience as a learning experience.

Don't let this inner ear disorder destroy your spirit. I know how you are feeling and it's hard to cope sometimes. But, you have to keep your spirits up. You have to keep living, and enjoying the things you once enjoyed.

If you were to just give up and say, "I'm dizzy…not today." Or, "Poor little me." You would be letting this disorder ruin your precious life. Don't let that happen. I felt sorry for myself in the beginning, but after about four months, I decided I just couldn't live like that. I began to walk, clean house and find new hobbies. I began to paint, and now have a beautiful painting of panda bears playing happily in a field hanging on my bedroom wall. I tried to teach myself to crochet…I'm still working on that one! I joined a weight and inch loss center where I work out at least three times a week. I'm losing weight, gaining muscle and I feel so much better not only physically, but mentally, too.

"A strong positive mental attitude will create more miracles than any wonder drug."
—*Patricia Neal*

Set Goals! And, Keep Dreaming! Even though the labyrinthitis caused delays in my life, such as not being able to lose weight, I continued to set realistic goals. These were goals that I could deal with at the time—that didn't include jumping around. I always write down my goals and scratch them out as I achieve them. My goals when I first got lab was to finish my Bachelor of Science degree, no matter what. I did. I also said that I would work on writing my first book. I did. Then, I began to make other goals, such as eating a healthier diet and exercise. I do. I eat a lot of salad and I no longer eat red meat. (That's just my own health choice.) I have new goals. I want to pursue my Master's degree in Education. I would like to become a teacher. I know that it is important to have goals and dreams. It gives us all a purpose. We all have a purpose in this life—and, it's not to deal with an inner ear disorder. So set those goals! Goals will keep you going…when you feel down…think of your goals.

Labyrinthitis will not run my life! I will keep my goals…Achieve my goals…And, set new goals…no matter what!

Start now by writing down some of your goals and dreams.

1. _____
2. _____
3. _____
4. _____
5. _____
6. _____
7. _____
8. _____
9. _____
10. _____

Get on the Internet…Go to the library.
Read all that you can about inner ear disorders and do research. The more you know about lab and other inner ear disorders, the better questions you can ask your care provider.

It's good to do your own research because some doctors brush this off and don't fully understand the effects it takes on a person's quality of life. Information is power. The more you know, the better care you can receive.

Find a health board to join and talk to others who have the same problem you do. It's very comforting to talk to others who are experiencing the same things you are. Some have even more information to give you. And, hearing others whose stories you can relate to, helps immensely. It also makes you feel good to hear about those people who HAD an inner ear disorder and are now feeling great, with no symptoms at all.

While surfing the Internet or reading, create a list of questions for your doctor…write them down before you forget…

1. _____
2. _____
3. _____
4. _____
5. _____
6. _____
7. _____
8. _____
9. _____
10. _____

"Ask your doctor anything that you need to. Don't worry about how the question may sound. Remember, there is no such thing as a dumb question. Express all of your concerns to maximize the care you receive."

Spend time with family and friends...

"The greatest HEALING therapy is friendship and love."
—*Hubert H. Humphrey, American Democratic Politician, Vice President*

When I'm with my family and friends, even on the worst of days...they seem to make me feel a whole lot better. My brother and sister can just about make me laugh no matter how terrible I feel.

You must surround yourself with loved ones to overcome this thing. Spending time playing with my children, or little nieces and nephews make me forget sometimes that I am sick.

I know that it is hard for some friends and family at this time, but close family and friends may be suffering just as well. No one who truly loves us wants to see us suffer. Loved ones may have to do more for things for you...some may not always understand your feelings and this is normal...I now understand them, too. I would never have been able to imagine these feelings of an inner ear disorder, if it were the other way around.

So go out and laugh. Have family and friends over for dinner. Go to birthday parties, and bowling night. Don't succumb to this illness. Learn to live with it, until it's gone. Don't let lab move in and take over.

Be thankful...

Be thankful that you are alive. There are some people who are worse off than you are. Some people are suffering a lot more than you. An inner ear disorder is not a terminal disease.

Go outside. Listen to the birds sing. Experience nature. Smile because you were allowed to wake up today.

Always...be thankful.

Create A Survival Kit...

A "Survival" kit can lift your spirits when you are feeling down. I created one for myself, but I think it would be a very nice, personal gift to create and give to a loved one, friend or a coworker who is dealing with an inner ear disorder.

Some ideas for your kit...

- An inspiring book, or novel
- Herbal tea (decaffeinated is best!)

- A nice mug (perhaps one with a smiley face)
- A picture of your loved ones, or a place you love. I love to look at a picture of myself when I was in Egypt standing in front of the great pyramids. I was so happy and excited. This picture takes me back to the days when I felt so good and didn't have any problems with my health.
- Candy (I keep mints and lemon drops, which are very calming.)
- Candles (I absolutely love the smell of vanilla, but lavender is also, a very calming scent.)
- A gift certificate for a massage. (Treat yourself to a stress relieving massage when you feel overwhelmed.)

My Journal

*** *I began my journal in April of 2003. I had been sick for six months and decided that I should start documenting experiences and journalizing my feelings on paper. It has been therapeutic keeping this journal.* ***

First entry. April 2003 (I had to back track)

September 15, 2002—Diagnosed with sinusitis—prescribed Augmentin. Felt a little dizzy, thought I just had the flu, or something.

October 3, 2002—Woke up at 4 a.m. with vertigo. Scared me out of my mind, went to the ER. They said I had fluid on my ear…middle ear infection???

October 7, 2002—Follow-up with my doctor—he said he thought I had labyrinthitis and it will go away.

October 22, 2002—Problem still there…when is it going away? Went to the doctor—he referred me to the ENT. I sat in the corner of the couch and wall and cried my eyes out…I couldn't catch my breath. I just can't stop crying.

November 12, 2002—ENT—he does hearing tests, epley maneuver and some balance test. He listened to my background and symptoms…that's how he came up with labyrinthitis. I was real dizzy at first, and then lost my balance. I also felt really lopsided when sitting. I mean it was terrible. He said it would take a while for it to go away.

January 2003—Starting to feel a little better. Decided to jump rope and got dizzy all over again. Damn! Went back to ENT scared. This time the ENT said that he thought I was getting better. Said that my labyrinth was coming back online and I had to get used to it being normal again. Noticed tinnitus at times.

February 2003—Had a MRI done just to resolve my brain tumor fears. I was fine. Everything was normal. Okay it was just my ear. Thank God. But, I still can't stop crying.

Between March 2003 and April 2003 (the day I began my journal) I have had little setbacks where some days I feel bad and think I'm going to go through this terrible thing from the beginning again. Still have some problems in certain positions. Looking up and down is no longer a problem, which was in the beginning.

I am feeling 99%-100% better. I still have tinnitus at times. Like when I'm hungry and my stomach growls—so will my right ear. Which is weird to me. Maybe the nerves in my ear are connected someway to those in my stomach. I'm not feeling as bad as I was. I am starting to feel more of an improvement.

I try to keep my hopes up; sometimes it's hard though—I'm just taking it day to day. I am on Zoloft because of the depression from this crap, but I am getting better with that too. I hope all of this will be a vague memory soon.

I know that every time I feel a little off after I've had good days—that it's a part of getting better. I know that this is just slow process, and when I feel a little off someday…it's because I am actually getting better. I think every time my ear makes a little progress—I tend to feel jacked up for a couple of weeks. I only say this because I feel weird this week after 3 weeks of feeling great, although during those 3 weeks I had really noticeable tinnitus. But, now that's improving. We'll see—time will tell.

July 15, 2003—Laby, Laby go away! Don't come back another day!

Today has been a good day for me. I'm going on 9 1/2 months and I can look up and down—left and right and all that. Sometimes during the day I feel just a little off, but…hey what's that??? I think there is a light at the end of this crazy tunnel.

July 24, 2003—After two days of feeling like crap, I feel better today…and yes, it has been raining the past two days so that's what I figure my setback has something to do with.

July 30, 2004—I had to be rushed to the ER again today. Last night I was feeling very nauseated. So, I went to sleep and woke up with vertigo for about 4 minutes. It scared the mess out of me. It was like 2:30 in the morning. Well, the vertigo went away but it was found that I have a bladder infection. It's been raining terribly here too, so I figure that might be part of the case. I am so mad…but, I feel better at the moment and it's 11 hours later. Hopefully, it's just an aftershock that will be nothing to worry about.

August 4, 2003—I was just thinking of what I could have done to give myself a "setback." I've been blaming it on this nasty, humid and rainy weather we have been having for a week...but, I have also been on a diet for 3 weeks and been exercising for 2 1/2 weeks straight. Whereas, before I didn't do anything but sit around and be depressed. I was too scared at first to exercise because I didn't want to trigger the dizzies. And, I've also lost 16 pounds from working out. I'm guessing this could have also put a wrench in the compensation process. But, I had my baby a year ago and never got to lose my pregnancy weight. I am going to continue my diet and exercise program because I need to get the rest of my body healthy...maybe from there everything will fall back into place. I just keep thinking that I'm going to get better because a guy my husband knows has had laby before for 6 weeks and he is completely normal again.

...I do know I will get better soon...It's so horrible that the brain has to fine-tune itself with every movement...You would think it would just remember. I am still feeling a little off, but I continue to exercise and now am learning Yoga. I'm not going to give up...I'm going to workout no matter how I'm feeling. Although, it's hard. Very hard at times.

August 10, 2003—Yesterday, I spent 10 hours at Busch Gardens amusement park. I felt good the whole time, too. (Except, for getting stung by a bee.) I felt a little dizzy and "off" when I sat down after about 3 hours of walking. But, it could have been the ride that was in front of me spinning around. That seemed to bother me. My hubby, brother-in-law's and nephew got on all of the rides. I passed on those of course. I didn't want to take any chances. Maybe, the next time I go to an amusement park, I'll get on a roller coaster—but I still don't have the nerve. A friend said that when I do decide to get on a roller coaster, it should be a kiddie ride. (Good advice.)

But, I felt good for the most part—so even with the setbacks I have—I am getting better, so it seems. I'm in month 10...

August 13, 2003—I woke up feeling okay but after reading on my side, I now feel off. It's also about to rain. I'm going to try and not stress about it. Maybe I gave my brain something new to relearn by reading on my side. I'm starting to think that I have BPPV as a result of lab. Depending on how I feel in another month—I will go back to the ENT and ask about the Epley Maneuver.

September 30, 2003—My ear problem is still here but seems to still be improving. I'll be going on a year Oct. 3. So, I'm hoping this will pass sooner than later.

I'm usually 97-98%. Still waiting on 100%. Some days though, like rainy days—are not as good for me. Oh gosh—the hurricane really played with my ear!

I've been working for a month and a 1/2 now. I was off for a year. I'm hanging in there—that's all I can possibly do. Found out that I am going on 9 weeks pregnant. YAYAAAY!! So, I'm having baby # 2 and can't wait. My morning sickness has been lasting all day, but seems to be subsiding. It's not as bad as the mess I'm going through now.

October 14, 2003—I was doing well, but…As much as I try to stay positive, I must say I'm tapping rock bottom with this lab again. I mean, I can certainly say I have been doing great. Working…driving…cleaning…shopping and lots of other things…I hit my one-year anniversary on Oct. 3, 2003 and I am actually feeling a little worse. I'm trying to get used to this crap…that it's probably around for much longer than a year. I am so depressed right now. I want to cry. I'm not as bad as I was—but it's just not going away. I stopped working the job I was at because I start a much better one, Nov. 3rd. I was wondering because I changed my schedule that I got messed up again. Like now, I get more sleep and I'm pregnant.

I want to cry and cry and cry.

October 15, 2003—I'm just going to continue to push on…until I get another good patch. My aunt tells me she had this same dizzy thing about 3 times in a 10-year period and she no longer has any problems. I was happy to hear that, but honestly want mine to leave me alone soon—real soon.

October 18, 2003—My right ear has been the problem ear for me…and I'm starting to notice that every month I get a WHOLE lot of earwax in my right ear that seems to trigger my bad phases again. If I clean my ear with peroxide and water—I get dizzy again. Although, this doesn't happen with my left ear. I clean my ear then have to wait about a week to feel 95% again. Today I'm still having somewhat a bad phase and I feel wax moving around, but I'm scared to clean it out. I wonder why this is happening???

October 19, 2003—I'm just going to trust Mother Nature and my body that it will heal itself.

October 28, 2003—After 3 weeks of a bad setback—I'm back to 99 percent. This is hell though—going back and forth, back and forth. I hope to get at 100 and stay soon.

October 29, 2003—I still have some wax, but seems like my ear eventually cleans itself. Then I seem to feel better. I'll go in for a follow up soon to get my ears looked at. I'll ask about the wax problem. I'm just content to be feeling good.

My morning sickness is gone, thankfully. (I still don't want to look at, or see Chinese food though) I was bleeding a little, but no worry, it was just from a pap test the doc did. I'm okay. I will be 14 weeks on Friday.

When I woke up, I was at 95%—now I'm at 98%. (It goes up and down…we had lots of rain—so I know that had something to do with it.)

But, in all honesty—I'm just so happy to feel as good as I do. Even if, not 100% yet. I'm happy. (At the moment)

October 30, 2003—I have been feeling really good. I was working in Aug and Sept of this year and was feeling great—I hardly ever noticed my lab prob. (GOOD THING) But, then I quit because that job didn't fit me too well and took a job that I am to start Nov. 3. Well, I've been off for an entire month—sitting around the house—not doing much. Well, I went to the mall today and drove myself and felt okay. But, now I'm home again and I can tell my brain is fine-tuning. I don't feel terrible, but I know that if I were to stay busy all the time—I would be really good by now.

I know now first hand that it is not good to stay in the house sitting around with this crap—it really makes this thing take longer to go away.

December 10, 2003-I hit 100% with this lab thing, finally last month…then, I got an external ear infection last week. OUCH!!!! I'm now getting over the pain, but had to get my ears professionally cleaned yesterday by the ENT. My problem ear took about 10 minutes to clean! I screamed so much at first, during the cleaning, that the doctor had to numb my bad ear, just to finish. Now, I feel a bit off and am not happy about it. I hope I get back to 100% again soon. I'm about 98% and I can really tell the difference when I have a setback.

December 28, 2003—I wonder if this lab stuff eventually gave me an outer ear infection? I just got over the most terrible, excruciating pain in my problem ear. I had to go on 2 courses of antibiotics. I'm okay right now. Hopefully this crap is working its way out and will finally leave me alone.

March 17, 2004—I know it's been a long time since I've written in my journal, but I feel good 99.8 percent of the time. I am still pregnant—due May 2 with a little boy. I had an ear infection in Dec/Jan but that's fine now. I am now optimistic that lab does go away—sometimes after a very long time, but I will not give up. I still go out sometimes and shoot hoops with hubby and exercise...walking especially.

May 28, 2004—I haven't written in awhile because I have been really busy with my new baby boy. (I also feel 100%, even though there are still times I feel a little weird.) Lonnie Jaden was born on April 27th. He was 8pds and 13ozs. His birth was easy and it didn't cause any problems with my compensation. Thank God.

October 26, 2004—

Early in the morning entry-

Well, it's been a little over two years now. I still feel just a bit off at times, but I have adjusted to my inner ear problem. My bad ear itches a lot now. (And, still gets a lot of wax.) For the past couple of days, I have been "bad." I took my pinky finger and have been scratching it. It itches a whole lot. I'm thinking I have, and have always had an allergy that causes this. I have been painting the house, which caused me to look up a lot. I noticed that I did this "normally."

I have been exercising like crazy. I walk on my treadmill for thirty minutes 5-6 times a week and I go to an inch loss center where I work out at least 3 times a week. I've lost 7 inches since September 15. I'm happy about that. I have a lot more weight to lose. My inner ear problem made me appreciate my health more and I want to keep my health, so even when I'm lazy—I will push myself up.

Later that night…

My ear is still itching badly and it feels like it's going to get infected again.

Poem

Dizzy Spell

Sometimes I fear that my ear may never heal
But, I know in my heart that it will
(Even though I'm having a dizzy spell)
When I hear the buzzing in my head
I tear up, sometimes I cry
(And, it just makes my dizziness worse)
I appear to be fine, but healthy and happy
I am not
(I'm having a dizzy spell)
I close my eyes, clear my mind
I tell myself, "to give it time"
(I still feel dizzy, but the "spell" won't last always)

—Gillian

Places that help...

Vestibular Disorders Association
P.O. Box 4467
Portland, OR 97208-4467
Telephone: 1-800-837-8428
E-mail: veda@vestibular.org
Website: www.vestibular.org

American Institute of Balance
11290 Park Boulevard
Seminole, Florida 33772
Telephone: 727-398-5728
Website: www.dizzy.com

American Hearing Research Foundation
8 South Michigan Avenue, Suite #814
Chicago, IL 60603-4539
Telephone: 312-726-9670
Website: www.american-hearing.org

American Tinnitus Association
PO Box 5
Portland, OR 97207
Telephone: 1-800-634-8978
Email: tinnitus@ata.org
Website: www.ata.org

American Academy of Otolaryngology-Head and Neck Surgery
AAO-HNS
One Prince Street
Alexandria, VA 22314
Telephone: 703-836-4444
Website: www.entnet.org

House Ear Institute
2100 West 3rd Street
Los Angeles, CA 90057
Telephone: 213-483-4431
Website: www.hei.org

Balance And Dizziness Disorders Society
Vancouver, BC, Canada
#325-5525 West Boulevard
Vancouver, B.C. Canada
V6M 3W6
Telephone: 604-878-8383
Email: info@balanceanddizziness.org
Website: www.balanceanddizziness.org

Acoustic Neuroma Association
600 Peachtree Pkwy, Suite 108
Cumming, GA 30041-6899
Telephone: (770) 205-8211
Email: ANAusa@aol.com
Website: http://anausa.org/

Another great website which was created by my buddies Emma and Ilia, who are also experiencing a dizzy spell is www.labyrinthitis.org.uk

References

Atlantic Coast Ear Specialists, P.C. Vincent Van Gogh and Dizziness. Scott, Janny.

Chicago Dizziness and Balance. Diagnosis and Treatment of Dizziness and Imbalance. http://www.dizziness-and-balance.com/cdb/testing.htm

eMedicine. Labyrinthitis. http://www.emedicine.com/emerg/topic290.htm

The Balance Care Center. Vestibular Injury. Compensation, Decompensation, and Failure to Compensate. Boismier, Thomas E.

University of Michigan Health System. Auditory-Brain Stem Response Testing for Adults. http://www.med.umich.edu/1libr/tests/testa14.htm

Vestibular Disorders Association. Labyrinthitis and Neurontis.
Vestibular Disorders Association. Vestibular Disorders: An Overview.

0-595-34044-X

Printed in the United Kingdom
by Lightning Source UK Ltd.
114749UKS00001B/381